A VISIT TO
WILLIAM BLAKE'S INN

POEMS FOR INNOCENT
AND EXPERIENCED
TRAVELERS

A VISIT TO

POEMS FOR INNOCENT

WILLIAM BLAKE'S INN

AND EXPERIENCED TRAVELERS

BY NANCY WILLARD

ILLUSTRATED BY
ALICE AND MARTIN PROVENSEN

HARCOURT BRACE JOVANOVICH, PUBLISHERS
SAN DIEGO   NEW YORK   LONDON

FOR RALPH, WHO BUILT THE INN,
AND FOR ERIC, WHO LOVES BLAKE

Design by Barbara DuPree Knowles

LIBRARY OF CONGRESS CATALOGING IN PUBLICATION DATA
Willard, Nancy. A visit to William Blake's inn.
SUMMARY: A collection of poems describing the curious menagerie
of guests who arrive at William Blake's inn.
1. Children's poetry, American. 2. Blake, William, 1757-1827,
in fiction, drama, poetry, etc.—Juvenile, literature.
[1. American poetry] I. Provensen, Alice. II. Provensen, Martin. III. Title.
PS3573.I444V5   811'.54   80-27403
ISBN 0-15-293822-2   AACRI
ISBN 0-15-293823-0   (VOYAGER/HBJ : PBK.)
PRINTED AND BOUND BY SOUTH CHINA PRINTING COMPANY, HONG KONG
D E F G H I J (pbk.)
G H I J

"Will you come?" said the Sun.
"Soon," said the Moon.
"How far?" said the Star.
"I'm there," said the Air.

CONTENTS

INTRODUCTION TO
WILLIAM BLAKE'S INN

I was seven and starting my second week in bed with the measles when I made the acquaintance of William Blake.

"Tell me a story about lions and tigers," I said to the babysitter. Although it was nearly nine o'clock, I had no desire to sleep.

Miss Pratt, the sitter, looked up at the ceiling on which my father had glued stars that glowed in the dark. Then she said, very softly, a poem that began:

> *Tyger, Tyger, burning bright*
> *In the forests of the night,*
> *What immortal hand or eye*
> *Could frame thy fearful symmetry?*

"Did you make that up?" I asked, astonished.

"No," said Miss Pratt. "William Blake made it up."

"Does he live close by?"

"He died nearly two hundred years ago," said Miss Pratt. "Lights off. I'm going downstairs."

Two days later there arrived in the mail a little book with wonderful pictures: *Songs of Innocence* and *Songs of Experience* by William Blake. I am almost sure Miss Pratt sent it. I say almost, because on the title page, in flourishing script, was the following inscription:

> *Poetry is the best medicine.*
> *Best wishes for a speedy recovery.*
> *yrs,*
> *William Blake*

NANCY WILLARD

WILLIAM BLAKE'S INN

FOR INNOCENT AND EXPERIENCED TRAVELERS

This inn belongs to William Blake
and many are the beasts he's tamed
and many are the stars he's named
and many those who stop and take
their joyful rest with William Blake.

Two mighty dragons brew and bake
and many are the loaves they've burned
and many are the spits they've turned
and many those who stop and break
their joyful bread with William Blake.

Two patient angels wash and shake
his featherbeds, and far away
snow falls like feathers. That's the day
good children run outside and make
snowmen to honor William Blake.

BLAKE'S WONDERFUL CAR
DELIVERS US WONDERFULLY WELL

The driver bowed and took my things.
He wore a mackintosh and wings.

He wore a mackintosh and boots
the tender green of onion shoots,

and on his cap, in dappled green,
was "Blake's Celestial Limousine."

My suitcases began to purr.
"Your luggage is excessive, sir.

All luggage must be carried flat
and worn discreetly on your hat

or served with mustard on a bun."
Alarmed, I said I hadn't one.

My suitcases, my fondest hopes
grew small and pale as envelopes.

"Now all aboard and all at ease.
I only carry whom I please."

Uneasily I stepped inside
and found the seats so green and wide,

the grass so soft, the view so far
it scarcely could be called a car,

rather a wish that only flew
when I climbed in and found it true.

A RABBIT REVEALS MY ROOM

When the rabbit showed me my room,
I looked all around for the bed.
I saw nothing there
but a shaggy old bear
who offered to pillow my head.

"I was hoping for blankets," I whispered.
"At home I've an afghan and sheet."
You will find my fur soft
as the hay in your loft,
and my paws make an admirable seat.

"I was hoping to waken at sunrise.
At home I've an excellent clock,
a lamp, and a glass
through which the hours pass,
and what shall I do for a lock?"

I will keep you from perilous starlight
and the old moon's lunatic cat.
When I blow on your eyes,
you will see the sun rise
with the man in the marmalade hat.

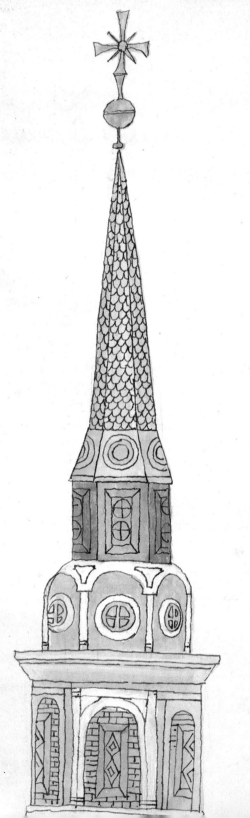

THE SUN AND MOON CIRCUS
SOOTHES THE WAKEFUL GUESTS

That night the tiger rose and said,
"What is this rumbling overhead
    that robs me of repose?"

To which the rabbit made reply,
"The moon is entering the sky,
    a-twirling on her toes."

The King of Cats sprang up in fright.
"What is this fitful flashing light
    that will not let me sleep?"

The rabbit said, with perfect tact,
"The sun is opening his act
    and crouching for a leap."

I rang the bell above my bed
so loud I thought I'd wake the dead.
    "Rabbit," I called, "come here!"

"No need," he said, "to cry and quake.
Two ancient friends of William Blake
    have come to bring us cheer."

Three sunflowers, in earthen beds,
stood up and slowly turned their heads
    with patience unsurpassed.

The old sun danced, the new moon sang,
I clapped my hands; the morning rang
as creatures clapped with paw and fang,
    and fell asleep at last.

The man in the marmalade hat
arrived in the middle of March,
equipped with a bottle of starch
to straighten the bends in the road, he said.
He carried a bucket and mop.
A most incommodious load, he said,
and he asked for a room at the top.

Now beat the gong and the drum!
Call out the keepers
and waken the sleepers.
The man in the marmalade hat has come!

The man in the marmalade hat
bustled through all the rooms,
and calling for dusters and brooms
he trundled the guests from their beds,
badgers and hedgehogs and moles.
Winter is over, my loves, he said.
Come away from your hollows and holes.

Now beat the gong and the drum!
Call out the keepers
And waken the sleepers.
The man in the marmalade hat has come!

THE KING OF CATS
ORDERS AN EARLY BREAKFAST

Roast me a wren to start with.
Then, Brisket of Basilisk Treat.
My breakfast is "on the house"?
What a curious place to eat!
There's no accounting for customs.
My tastes are simple and few,
a fat mole smothered in starlight
and a heavenly nine-mouse stew.

I shall roll away from the table
looking twice my usual size.
"Behold the moon!" you will whisper.
"How marvelous his disguise.
How like the King of Cats he looks,
how similar his paws
and his prodigious appetite—
why, in the middle of the night
he ate, with evident delight,
a dozen lobster claws."

"Where did you sleep last night, Wise Cow?
Where did you lay your head?"

"I caught my horns on a rolling cloud
and made myself a bed,

and in the morning ate it raw
on freshly buttered bread."

TWO SUNFLOWERS

MOVE INTO THE YELLOW ROOM

"Ah, William, we're weary of weather,"
said the sunflowers, shining with dew.
"Our traveling habits have tired us.
Can you give us a room with a view?"

They arranged themselves at the window
and counted the steps of the sun,
and they both took root in the carpet
where the topaz tortoises run.

THE WISE COW
MAKES *Way, Room,* AND *Believe*

The Rabbit cried, "Make *Way!*
Make *Way* for William Blake!
Let our good poet pass."
The Wise Cow said, "Alas!
Alack! How shall I make
a thing I've never seen?
To one that lives on grass
what's good is green.
Therefore I must make *Way*
of grass and hay,
a nest where he can nap
like fieldmice in a cap."

The Rabbit cried, "Make *Room!*
Make *Room* for the marmalade man!
He is mopping and mapping the floors.
He is tidying cupboards and drawers."
The Wise Cow said, "Can I
make *Room* and *Way* together?
To one that lives outdoors
what's good is weather.
Therefore I must make *Room*
like a bright loom.
The marmalade man can weave
good weather, I believe."

The Rabbit cried, "Make *Believe,*
and make it strong and clear
that I may enter in
with all my kith and kin."
The Wise Cow said, "My dear,
Believe shall be a boat
having both feet and fins.
We'll leave this quiet moat.
We'll welcome great and small
with *Ways* and *Rooms* for all,
and for our captain let us take
the noble poet, William Blake."

He gave silver shoes to the rabbit
and golden gloves to the cat
and emerald boots to the tiger and me
and boots of iron to the rat.

He inquired, "Is everyone ready?
The night is uncommonly cold.
We'll start on our journey as children,
but I fear we will finish it old."

He hurried us to the horizon
where morning and evening meet.
The slippery stars went skipping
under our hapless feet.

"I'm terribly cold," said the rabbit.
"My paws are becoming quite blue,
and what will become of my right thumb
while you admire the view?"

"The stars," said the cat, "are abundant
and falling on every side.
Let them carry us back to our comforts.
Let us take the stars for a ride."

"I shall garland my room," said the tiger,
"with a few of these emerald lights."
"I shall give up sleeping forever," I said.
"I shall never part day from night."

The rat was sullen. He grumbled
he ought to have stayed in his bed.
"What's gathered by fools in heaven
will never endure," he said.

Blake gave silver stars to the rabbit
and golden stars to the cat
and emerald stars to the tiger and me
but a handful of dirt to the rat.

Fire, you handsome creature, shine.
Let the hearth where I confine
your hissing tongues that rise and fall
be the home that warms us all.

When the wind assaults my doors
every corner's cold but yours.
When the snow puts earth to sleep
let your bright behavior keep

all these little pilgrims warm.
They who never did you harm
raise their paws a little higher
and toast their toes, in praise of fire.

THE MARMALADE MAN
MAKES A DANCE TO MEND US

Tiger, Sunflowers, King of Cats,
Cow and Rabbit, mend your ways.
I the needle, you the thread—
follow me through mist and maze.

Fox and hound, go paw in paw.
Cat and rat, be best of friends.
Lamb and tiger, walk together.
Dancing starts where fighting ends.

THE KING OF CATS
SENDS A POSTCARD TO HIS WIFE

Dearest Wife and helpmeet
Keep your whiskers, meat and c
Have you set the kittens

Keep your whiskers crisp and clean.
Do not let the mice grow lean.
Do not let yourself grow fat
like a common kitchen cat.

Have you set the kittens free?
Do they sometimes ask for me?
Is our catnip growing tall?
Did you patch the garden wall?

Clouds are gentle walls that hide
gardens on the other side.
Tell the tabby cats I take
all my meals with William Blake,

lunch at noon and tea at four,
served in splendor on the shore
at the tinkling of a bell.
Tell them I am sleeping well.

Tell them I have come so far,
brought by Blake's celestial car,
buffeted by wind and rain,
I may not get home again.

Take this message to my friends.
Say the King of Catnip sends
to the cat who winds his clocks
a thousand sunsets in a box,

to the cat who brings the ice
the shadows of a dozen mice
(serve them with assorted dips
and eat them like potato chips),

and to the cat who guards his door
a net for catching stars, and more
(if with patience he abide):
catnip from the other side.

William, William, writing late
by the chill and sooty grate,
what immortal story can
make your tiger roar again?

When I was sent to fetch your meat
I confess that I did eat
half the roast and all the bread.
He will never know, I said.

When I was sent to fetch your drink,
I confess that I did think
you would never miss the three
lumps of sugar by your tea.

Soon I saw my health decline
and I knew the fault was mine.
Only William Blake can tell
tales to make a tiger well.

Now I lay me down to sleep
with bear and rabbit, bird and sheep.
If I should dream before I wake,
may I dream of William Blake.

BLAKE TELLS THE TIGER
THE TALE OF THE TAILOR

There was a tailor built a house
of wool of bat and fur of mouse,
of moleskin suede, the better part
of things that glimmer, skim and dart.

Of wood and stone the man professed
his ignorance. He said, "It's best
to work with what I know.
Shears, snip. Thread, go.
I'll have a house in the morning."

The tailor and his wife moved in
and lined it well with onionskin.
Of velveteen they made the chairs,
and snails' feet and comets' hairs.

Of bricks and boards the man professed
his ignorance. He said, "It's best
to work with what I know.
Shears, snip. Thread, go.
I'll have a house in the morning."

And when that pair lay down to sleep,
cries and chirps conspired to keep
the tailor and his wife awake.
"Husband, since we cannot take

fur and fury, wool and wings
back to those who lost these things,
back to those from whom we stole
wool of bat and skin of mole,
let us leave this house and take
rooms at the inn of William Blake."

Of ghostly griefs, the man professed
his ignorance. He said, "It's best
to work with what I know.
Shears, snip. Thread, go.
We'll go to Blake's in the morning."

That night the winds of April blew
the tailor's house apart, askew,
and the wet wind who once went bare
wore wool of bat and comet's hair.

He made their bed of robins' wings
caught, with other flying things,
in a low trap of twigs and lime.
It was the tailor's own design.

On windy days and moonless nights,
Blake wears a suit of shifting lights.
The tailor now has grown so clever
he stitches light and dark together.

Of nails and knotholes he professed
his ignorance. He said, "It's best
to work with what I know.
Shears, snip. Thread, go.
I'll have a house in the morning."

"Now sun and sparrows, take your rest.
And farewell, friendly trees. It's best
to work with what I know.
Shears, snip. Thread, go.
All things are new in the morning."

My adventures now are ended.
I and all whom I befriended
from this holy hill must go
home to lives we left below.

Farewell cow and farewell cat,
rabbit, tiger, sullen rat.
To our children we shall say
how we walked the Milky Way.

You whose journeys now begin,
if you reach a lovely inn,
if a rabbit makes your bed,
if two dragons bake your bread,
rest a little for my sake,
and give my love to William Blake.

BLAKE'S ADVICE TO TRAVELERS

He whose face gives no light
will never become a star.

William Blake

—from "Proverbs of Hell,"
The Marriage of Heaven and Hell
by William Blake